The Philippines

by Holly Longworth

Consultant: Marjorie Faulstich Orellana, PhD
Professor of Urban Schooling
University of California, Los Angeles

BEARPORT
PUBLISHING

New York, New York

Credits

Cover, © Tony Magdaraog/Shutterstock and Pichugin Dmitry/Shutterstock; TOC, © arjanhuijzer/iStock; 4, © freeartist/123RF; 5T, © donsimon/Shutterstock; 5B, © tykhyi/123RF; 7T, © Seam3810/iStock; 7B, © Elena Yakusheva/Shutterstock; 8–9, © soft_light/Shutterstock; 9B, © strmko/iStock; 10, © EyeEm/iStock; 11, © donsimon/Shutterstock; 12–13, © Simon Gurney/123RF; 13, © Edwin Verin; 14, © Viktar Malyshchyts/Shutterstock; 14–15, © Adwo/Shutterstock; 16, © donsimon/Shutterstock; 17, © Hemis/Alamy; 18, © ArtPhaneuf/iStock; 18–19, © OlegD/Shutterstock; 20–21, © ROLEX DELA PENA/EPA/Newscom; 22, © Art Phaneuf Photography/Shutterstock; 23, © Tim Graham/Alamy; 24, © Hrlumanog/Dreamstime; 25, © Junpinzon/Dreamstime.com; 26, © imagegallery2/Alamy; 26–27, © Hrlumanog/Dreamstime; 28, © View Apart/Shutterstock; 29T, © Hanhanpeggy/Dreamstime; 29B, © irin-k/Shutterstock; 30 (T to B), © fourleaflover/Shutterstock, © Tony Magdaraog/Shutterstock, © Asaf Eliason/Shutterstock, and © OlegDoroshenko/depositphotos; 31 (T to B), © KieferPix/Shutterstock, © Borisoff/Shutterstock, © Elena Kalistratova/Shutterstock, © Quick Shot/Shutterstock, and © Juhku/Shutterstock; 32, © Solodov Alexey/Shutterstock.

Publisher: Kenn Goin
Editor: Jessica Rudolph
Creative Director: Spencer Brinker
Design: Debrah Kaiser

Library of Congress Cataloging-in-Publication Data

Longworth, Holly, author.
  The Philippines / by Holly Longworth
      pages cm — (Countries we come from)
  Summary: "In this book, readers learn what it is like living in the Philippines"— Provided by publisher.
  Audience: Ages 4–8.
  Includes bibliographical references and index.
  ISBN 978-1-62724-855-6 (library binding) — ISBN 1-62724-855-2 (library binding)
  1. Philippines—Pictorial works—Juvenile literature. I. Title.
  DS656.2.L66 2016
  959.9—dc23
                                  2015008788

For more information, write to Bearport Publishing Company, Inc., 45 West 21st Street, Suite 3B, New York, New York 10010. Printed in the United States of America.

10 9 8 7 6 5 4 3 2

Contents

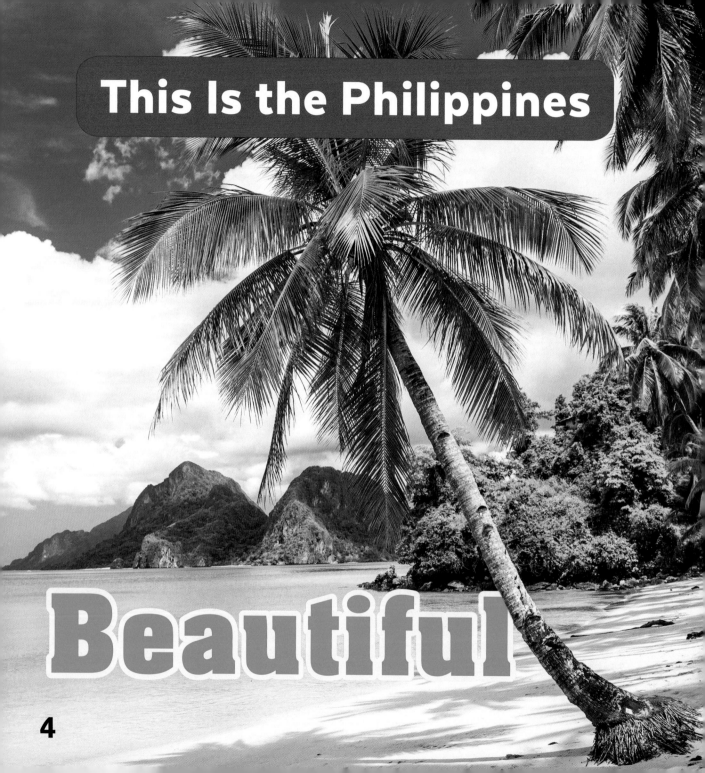

This Is the Philippines

Beautiful

BUSY

HILLY

The Philippines is a country in Asia.

It's made up of more than 7,000 islands.

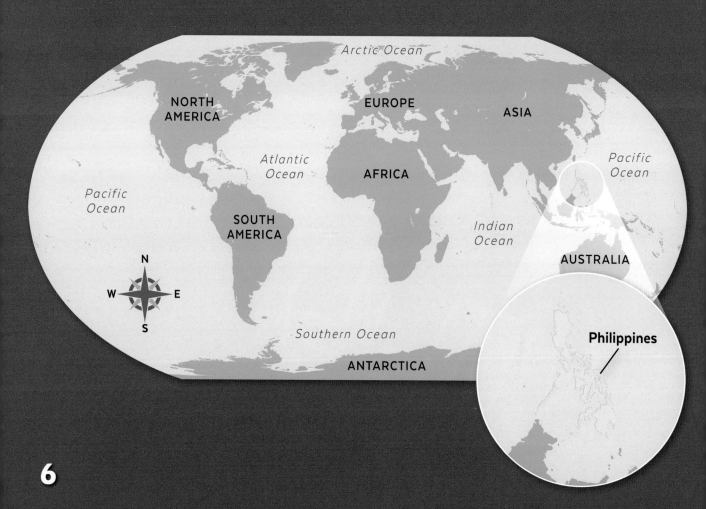

People who
live there are
called Filipinos
or Pilipinos.

The Philippines has beautiful beaches.

Some beaches have white sand.
Others have black or pink sand.

Near the beaches,
colorful fish swim
around **coral reefs**.

coral reef

The Philippines has lots of mountains.

Some of the mountains are volcanoes.

Sometimes the volcanoes **erupt**.

The weather on the islands is warm and rainy.

There are **rain forests** in the wettest areas.

Many animals live in the rain forests, such as tarsiers. The tarsiers' huge eyes help them to see at night.

13

Some Filipinos work on farms.

They grow lots of different foods.

Coconuts grown in the Philippines are sold all over the world.

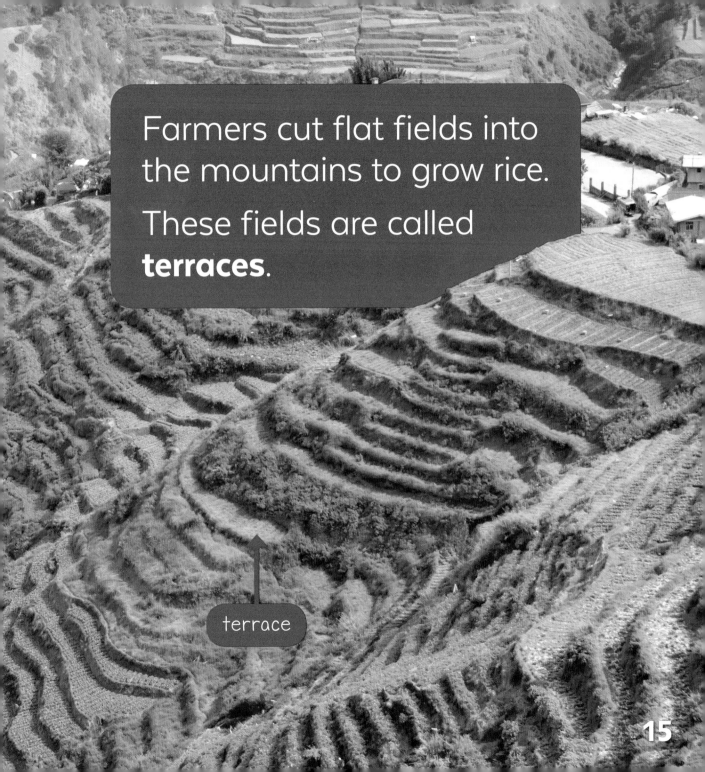

Farmers cut flat fields into the mountains to grow rice.

These fields are called **terraces**.

terrace

There are many big cities in the Philippines.

Manila is the country's **capital**.

More than one million people live in Manila.

How do people get around?

Some Filipinos travel in jeepneys.

Jeepneys are colorful buses.

People use boats or bridges to get from island to island.

jeepney

19

The Philippines has a long history.

People have lived there for thousands of years.

The country was once ruled by Spain, then by the United States.

Filipinos fought for their freedom. Today, the Philippines is its own country.

Filipinos celebrating their freedom with a parade

21

People speak many languages in the Philippines.

Most people speak Tagalog or Filipino.

This is how you say *yes* in Tagalog:

Oo (OH-oh)

This is how you say *thank you*:

Salamat (sahl-AH-maht)

Many Filipinos also speak English.

fish market

What do Filipinos like to eat?

They eat lots of rice and fish.

People buy fresh fish in markets.

Adobo is a popular dish. It's made by cooking meat or fish in a vinegar sauce.

Filipinos celebrate many holidays.

On All Saints' Day, people remember loved ones who have died.

Some people decorate graves with candles and flowers.

For fun, Filipinos play sports such as basketball.

Basketball is played all over the country.

Soccer is also very popular.

29

Fast Facts

Capital city: Manila

Population of the Philippines:
More than 98 million

Main languages: Tagalog and Filipino

Money: Philippine peso

Major religion: Roman Catholic

Nearby countries include:
China and Vietnam

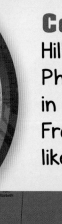

Cool Fact: The Chocolate Hills are a group of hills in the Philippines that are covered in brownish—green grass. From far away, the hills look like mounds of chocolate!

Glossary

capital (KAP-uh-tuhl) the city where a country's government is based

coral reefs (KORE-uhl REEFS) rock-like structures formed from the skeletons of sea animals called coral polyps

erupt (i-RUPT) to send out lava, ash, steam, and gas from a volcano

rain forests (RAYN FORE-ists) warm places where many trees grow and lots of rain falls

terraces (TER-iss-iz) raised, flat platforms of land with sloping sides

31

Index

Read More

Burgan, Michael. *Philippines (Countries Around the World).* Chicago: Heinemann (2012).

Kalman, Bobbie. *Spotlight on the Philippines (Spotlight on My Country).* New York: Crabtree (2011).

Learn More Online

To learn more about the Philippines, visit
www.bearportpublishing.com/CountriesWeComeFrom

About the Author

Holly Longworth lives in New York and enjoys reading, writing, and traveling.